CW00820562

The meandering waterside at Blakeney.
Right: the beautiful medieval village of Lavenham.

EAST ANGLIA

John Potter

MYRIAD

Right: Dedham Hall. The pretty village of Dedham is located on the Essex bank of the river Stour opposite Flatford and has many associations with the painter John Constable. Dedham Hall was the old grammar school where Constable studied.

Far right: the half-timbered Marlborough Head Hotel in Dedham town centre.

Below: Flatford Mill, where Constable grew up is the subject of many of his most famous paintings.

Left: Colchester Castle.

Right: Tymperleys Clock Museum is housed in a 15th-century timber-framed building.

Below: Colchester Town Hall's 162ft Victoria Tower dominates the high street. The statue at the top is of St Helena, patron saint of Colchester.

Left and right: the historic hill town of Maldon stands at the head of the Blackwater Estuary. It is home to many historic Thames sailing barges which can be seen regularly moored up by the Jolly Sailor Inn at the quay. Below: a dinghy at nearby Mistley.

Left: restored wooden sail lofts at Tollesbury – often referred to as the village of the "Plough and Sail".

Right: Clacton and its famous pier, built in the late 1900s when Peter Schuyler Bruff, an engineer and manager of the Eastern Union Railway, constructed a pier which gave large boats from London the ability to moor and unload passengers.

Right: the annual gathering of Morris Men at Thaxted, the spiritual home of Morris dancing.

Below: picturesque almshouses in the churchyard of St John the Baptist in Thaxted. In the distance is the Thaxted tower mill.

Right and below: the picture postcard village of Finchingfield is situated between Sible Hedingham and Thaxted on the Braintree to Saffron Walden road. The village has a pretty green, a duckpond and a windmill, together with several medieval houses known as *cabbaches*. Many of the cottages have pargetting, a type of decorative plasterwork on their walls which is very characteristic of the area.

Right: the quay along the river Alde at Snape Maltings.

Below: *Scallop*, on Aldeburgh beach, a tribute to the composer Benjamin Britten who made his home in the town.

Below: Orford is an unspoiled fishing and tourist village on the estuary of the river Alde. Opposite Orford, on the far side of the river Alde, lies Orford Ness, a long spit stretching 10 miles up the coast to Aldeburgh.

Left: Southwold lighthouse stands in the middle of this unique and elegant seaside town. The town is virtually an island, bounded by the North Sea to the east, the river Blyth and Southwold harbour to the south-west, and Buss Creek to the north.

Below: the pretty beach at Southwold has many brightly painted fishermen's and bathers' huts.

Above and right: just across the river Blyth from Southwold, Walberswick was once a thriving trading port dealing in fish, bacon, cheese, corn and timber.

Left: the medieval village of Lavenham lies a few miles north-east of Sudbury and is famous for its collection of half-timbered buildings. During the late middle ages it was one of the wealthiest towns in Britain thanks to the prosperity of the local wool trade.

Above and left: situated 18 miles north-east of Ipswich, Framlingham has an attractive market square, Market Hill, which features the old water pump used to fill water carts when houses in the town lacked their own supply. The castle is a magnificent landmark with dramatic views across the mere.

Left: King's College, Cambridge. The city centre is dominated by many of the university's beautiful historic buildings.

Right: no visit to Cambridge is complete without a trip in a punt.

Below: the famous Baron of Beef pub in Bridge Street, Cambridge, a short distance from Magdalene Bridge.

Left: St Neots, the largest town in Cambridgeshire, is situated on the Great Ouse, which meanders peacefully through the town and forms the border with the historic county of Huntingdonshire. Below: the quayside at Ely has been beautifully restored with inns and restaurants.

Right: Ely Cathedral, is known locally as "the ship of the Fens" because of its slender tower which looms above the surrounding flat countryside. The eight-sided tower in the centre of the church is the only Gothic dome in existence and the cathedral is set within the walls of a Benedictine monastery.

Right: Sandringham, the beautiful country retreat of the Queen and the Duke of Edinburgh, has been passed down through four generations of the royal family.

Below: West Newton primary school on the Sandringham estate.

Above: HRH the Prince of Wales and the Duchess of Cornwall open the flower show at Sandringham. This popular event attracts thousands of visitors to the royal estate each July.

Above: Houghton Hall, home of Britain's first prime minister, Sir Robert Walpole, is set in 350 acres of fine gardens and parkland in which a large herd of rare, white fallow deer roam freely.

Left: the picture postcard village of Great Massingham, east of King's Lynn, has a number of attractive large ponds, These were used as fishponds by the 11th century Augustinian abbey which once stood here.

Above: the peaceful village of Castle Acre a few miles north of Swaffham is famous for the twin ruins of Castle Acre castle and Castle Acre priory.

Left: situated midway between Sandringham and Houghton Hall in north Norfolk, the tiny village of Anmer has an enviable location.

Below: Blickling Hall is one of England's finest Jacobean houses. A short distance north-west of Aylsham it is famous for its long gallery, fine furniture, superb library, pictures and tapestries.

Left: England's oldest lavender farm at Caley Mill, Heacham between King's Lynn and the seaside resort of Hunstanton.

Right: south of Hunstanton on the north Norfolk coast, Snettisham is a pretty village with views across the Wash towards Lincolnshire.
An important RSPB nature reserve is situated two miles to the west. In the depths of winter thousands of geese can be seen commuting between their safe roosts in the Wash and nearby farmland.

Above: the Old Lighthouse in the picturesque village of Old Hunstanton. Constructed in 1844 this prominent landmark is one of the many beacons or lantern lights which have been used to warn shipping of dangers along this coast for centuries.

Left: the three villages of Brancaster, Brancaster Staithe and Burnham Deepdale form a more or less continuous line along the marshland fringing Brancaster Bay. Legend has it that England's greatest naval commander, Lord Horatio Nelson, sailed his first boat at Brancaster Staithe. The bust of Nelson (inset) is located in the chancel of All Saints church where his father was rector.

Right: the Tower Mill at Burnham Overy Staithe.

Above: beach huts at Wells-next-the-Sea, a charming, historic seaside resort brimming with character and atmosphere.

Left: the seal colony at Blakeney Point – a world-renowned nature reserve and seal sanctuary.

Right: the silting of the estuary at Blakeney has left a fascinating landscape of marshes, sand hills and mud banks, with many creeks and channels.

Left and above: Cromer. Situated on a cliff top overlooking fine sandy beaches, Cromer is north Norfolk's premier seaside resort. The town's elegant Edwardian pier was one of the first "pleasure" piers to be built in the 20th century and celebrated its centenary in 2001.

Right: Hickling Broad, with its traditional reed-thatched boat houses, presents an evocative Broadland scene – complete with a pretty village. The large water-filled Broads are connected by over 200 miles of navigable rivers, dykes and cuts. Although this watery region straddles both Norfolk and Suffolk it is known as the Norfolk Broads. There are over 50 Broads but only 13 of them are usually open to the fleets of pleasurecraft which ply these waterways.

Left: Horsey Mill, a fully restored drainage windpump, stands proudly beside the edge of Horsey Mere between Sea Palling and Winterton-on-Sea.

Below: there are three restored windmills at How Hill. The evocative Turf Fen windmill was erected in 1875 to drain Horning marshes into the river Ant.

Left: the magnificent cathedral of the Holy and Undivided Trinity in Norwich dominates the city centre and is the focus of spiritual life in Norfolk.

Above: the castle at Norwich was originally a wooden motte and bailey construction built by William the Conqueror in 1067. Today the castle serves as the city museum.
Right: the impressive two-storey cloisters of Norwich Cathedral played a key part in the life of the original Benedictine monastery.